SO-BJF-252

DISCARD

55959

917
.16
00222
Cor

Cormier, Roméo.
   Image of Acadia. Photos. by Roméo
Cormier. Introd. by Léon Thériault.
Toronto, Oxford University Press, 1980.
   86 p. ill., map.

1. Acadia – Description and travel – Views.
2. Maritime Provinces – Description and
travel – Views. I. Title.
0195403304   1025244

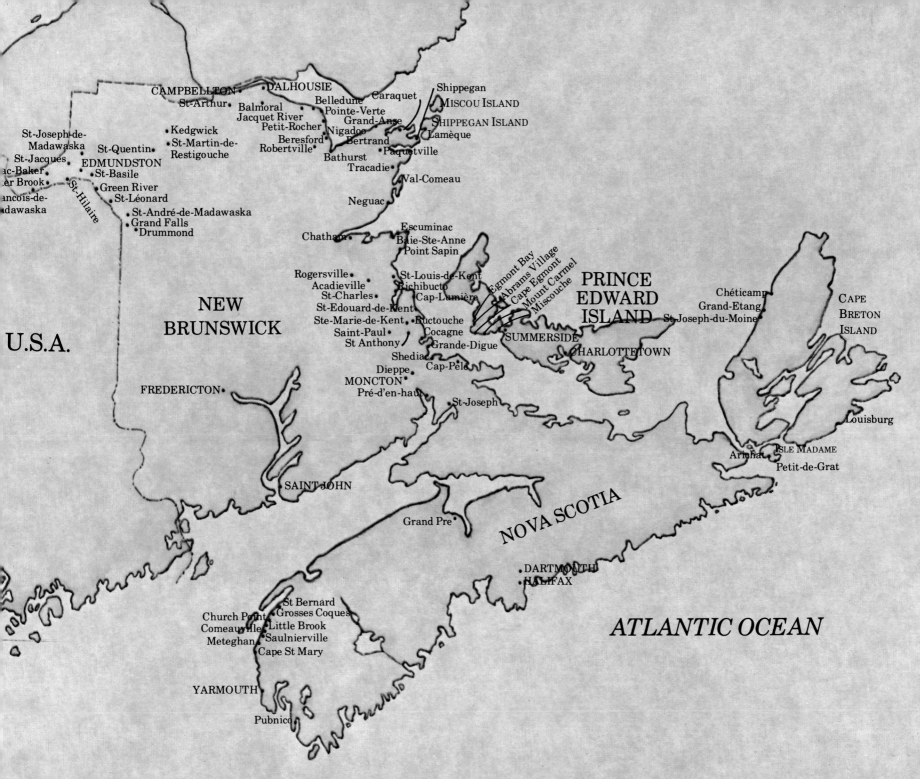

CAMPBELLTON • • DALHOUSIE
St-Arthur • Belledune Caraquet Shippegan
Balmoral • Pointe-Verte MISCOU ISLAND
Jacquet River Grand-Anse
Kedgwick Petit-Rocher Nigadoo SHIPPEGAN ISLAND
St-Joseph-de- • St-Martin-de- Beresford Bertrand • Lamèque
Madawaska St-Quentin • Restigouche Robertville •
St-Jacques EDMUNDSTON Bathurst • Paquetville
ac-Baker • St-Basile Tracadie
er Brook • Green River Val-Comeau
ançois-de- St-Léonard
dawaska • St-André-de-Madawaska Neguac
St-Hilaire • Grand Falls
• Drummond Escuminac
Chatham • Baie-Ste-Anne
Point Sapin
Rogersville Egmont Bay PRINCE
NEW Acadieville St-Louis-de-Kent Abrams Village EDWARD
BRUNSWICK St-Charles Richibucto Cape Egmont ISLAND
St-Edouard-de-Kent Cap-Lumière Mount Carmel
Ste-Marie-de-Kent Buctouche Miscouche Chéticamp
Saint-Paul Cocagne SUMMERSIDE Grand-Etang CAPE
St Anthony Grande-Digue St-Joseph-du-Moine BRETON
U.S.A. Shediac CHARLOTTETOWN ISLAND
Dieppe Cap-Pelé
FREDERICTON • MONCTON
Pré-d'en-haut
• St-Joseph Louisburg
Arichat ISLE MADAME
Petit-de-Grat
SAINT JOHN

NOVA SCOTIA
Grand Pre •
ATLANTIC OCEAN

• DARTMOUTH
• HALIFAX

St Bernard
Church Point Grosses Coques
Comeauville Little Brook
Meteghan Saulnierville
Cape St Mary

YARMOUTH

Pubnico

ames as shown in the *Maritime Provinces* map of the Surveys and Mapping Branch, Department of Energy, Mines and Resources, Ottawa

Image of Acadia

Photographs by Roméo Cormier

Introduction by Léon Thériault

Toronto
Oxford University Press
1980

to Alma

Designed by *Fortunato Aglialoro*
© Oxford University Press (Canadian Branch) 1980
ISBN 0-19-540330-4
Printed in Hong Kong by
EVERBEST PRINTING COMPANY LIMITED

List of Plates

Preface

by *Roméo Cormier*

This selection of photographs comes from a wish that I have in common with many of my fellow countrymen — to picture in the round the living reality of Acadia.

Settled in this part of the country for nearly four centuries, but dispersed through the length and breadth of three Canadian provinces, Acadians feel today more than ever the need to form a clear perception of their homeland. It was in the hope that I could help to meet this need that I undertook to travel throughout Acadia, to get to know how things are with us, and to share in the riches of Acadia, both natural and human.

The images that follow do not so much try to recall our past as to show our profound attachment to the soil and the sea. We have lived here for 375 years and our attachment to this land is such that we already look forward to our four hundredth anniversary in Acadia.

Introduction

by Léon Thériault

*I named this the River of Cockaigne [the land of milk and honey],
because I found such an abundance of good food there during
the week that I was kept there by bad weather and because
everybody was so sated with game and fish that they could eat no more....
The country is as pleasurable as the food, a level terrain covered
with very beautiful trees, as notable for their girth as for their height,
and of every species that I could name. There are also great meadows
along the river, which is navigable for five or six leagues inland,
the rest being passable only by canoe, and here are to be found
many more pines than other kinds of trees.*

Nicolas Denys, *Geographical and Historical Description of the Northern American Coasts.
With the Natural History of the Country*. Paris, 1672. Volume 1 pp. 173-4

THE PLACE-NAME ACADIA comes from the word arcady or arcadia, a term of Greek mythology that denotes the ideal land of rural peace and happiness. Instead, what troubles has Acadia known! First European colony in North America, founded by France as early as 1604, Acadia was continually at war with the British colonies to the south. In 1755 the British expelled the Acadians and in 1763 the French gave up the entire region to their British rivals.

The hold of their land on these early forefathers was such that many of those who had been exiled returned to found a new Acadia, though under British rule. Today sixteen per cent of the inhabitants of the Maritime provinces of Canada are French speaking, most of them tracing their descent back to the first pioneer Acadians.

Most Acadians today live along the coasts, as they did in the first days of the colony; the daily work of these fishermen, lumbermen, and farmers, as in the past, is in harvesting the riches of nature. However, a growing number of industrial workers, technicians, artists, and writers attests to a diversity and dynamism in Acadian life that is becoming more and more pronounced.

The Acadians are bound by their language, their history, and their common beliefs. But the roots of the Acadian people are also imbedded in the soil, in the land itself. Land is among the most precious endowments of a people, for it is the land that ensures survival, shapes the collective hopes, bears witness to the labours of the past, and holds the promise of the future. If one can study a people by the scrutiny of their archives, one can also tell a great deal about them by getting to know their surroundings.

The images presented here by Roméo Cormier are indeed a commentary on the Acadian people and on the land in which they live. Despite the use of a modern medium, photography, the intent and the work call to mind the classic descriptions of Marc Lescarbot, Nicolas Denys and Dièreville, who were the exponents of Acadia in former times. We are now in a position to judge whether, three hundred and seventy-five years after its foundation, Acadia has preserved the essentials of its magic charm.

5

6

7

13

15

17

18

23

24

27

28

30

31

3.

35

40

42

46   47

48   49

52

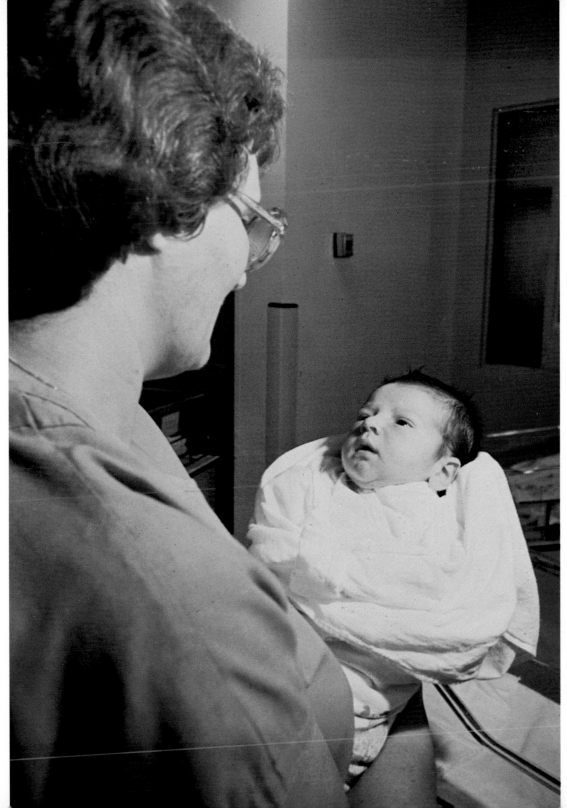

53

54

57

60

62

9

70   71

7

74   75

▷86